I0485479

Freelance Writing

Learn to Earn
From your Writing Skills

By
Meenakshi Narang

I

Table of Contents

INTRODUCTION

We all want to meet professional success. However, sometimes we don't get a chance at becoming what we always wanted to become in life. Unexpected changes in life like motherhood, disability, getting laid off from your job or any other responsibility might make it difficult for you to pursue the career that you initially intended to. Take a decision if you want to sit and mope around about the change or shine through it.

If you have been in such situations or something similar, this is the time for you to take a decisive step and decide. For those who want to establish an identity for themselves, look at freelance writing as a lucrative career option.

This is no way a suggestion that freelance writing is a last resort career option. Many have quitted their high-income jobs to pursue their passion for writing. And trust us when we say this, they still maintain their high income, by working as per their convenience and on their terms.

The bottom line here is Freelance writing is one of the most lucrative self-employment business ideas. For those aspiring to be freelance writers or those who want to earn an extra buck while taking care of the babies, here is a simple and honest effort to understand the intricacies and nuances of freelance writing. This will guide you to set a new goal and create a career and an identity for yourself while addressing your personal commitments too.

Chapter 1: Freelance Writing

The term freelance writer is known to many. Rather some of you might also personally know someone who is a freelance writer. So the one question that must have crossed your mind is – What exactly does this person do?

Well, let us simplify the term 'freelance writer' for you. Of course, it is pretty self-explanatory. A freelance writer is a person who takes on writing work like copies, blogs, articles, internet content, E-books and the likes. These are usually published on websites, BlogSpot, magazine, books, brochures, manuals, posters, newspapers or any other print and social media. A freelance writer need not be someone who has a journalism degree or done some courses about writing skills. Anyone who has the flair to write, a strong command over a language, has strong grammar skills and can weave stories or content together can become a freelance writer.

There are infinite options and opportunities in terms of work for freelance writers and, believe it or not, you can get rewarded handsomely for the work you do. Of course for you to get the kind of work traffic and money that we are talking about, you need to establish yourself as a writer of an impressive caliber. Once done, your journey as a freelance writer will be amazing and rewarding.
⁇

What It Takes To Become A Freelance Writer?

The beauty of being a freelance writer is you don't have to be qualified in a certain degree, nor do you have to be a subject matter expert.

As long as you have a way with words and are willing to put the much needed time in research you can take up the challenge of being a freelance writer. You can become a freelance writer if:

- You have a strong command in a certain language (preferably English)
- You have excellent grammar skills
- You can interest the readers with your words
- You are willing to research about any topic or learn about new things happening in the world

- You have that talent and an eye for detail that is needed (you don't want to mislead people with your writing)
- You are interested and passionate about writing

If you think you can manage to click on all of the above options; then believe me, becoming a freelance writer is not difficult.

Being a Writer: A Rollercoaster Ride

Every career comes with its sets of pros and cons. You may be a high flying entrepreneur, but quality time may be hard to come by for you. Similarly, a clerk at a small firm may have ample time with family, but the paycheck may not be very lucrative. In the same way being a freelance writer, too comes with its sets of pros and cons. Let us take a look at them both, so it would be easy for you to determine whether a freelance writing job is ideal for you or not.

There are several highpoints of being a freelance writer. Here are some common reasons why being a freelance writer could be much better than your regular 9 to 5 job.

Be Your Own Boss – Most people keep changing jobs because they are not happy with their immediate bosses. It is said that, no one leaves the company but their bosses. In your career span, you must have encountered a boss who made it difficult for you to continue working. Imagine a scenario where there is no boss. Better yet, imagine a scenario where you are your boss. Interesting!

Convenient Working – Though convenient working holds different connotations for different people, here we are implying working as per convenience. The biggest pro is you work from the comfort of your home. You don't have to brave the harsh weather to reach the office. No traffic, no alarm clocks (no waking up forcibly or after that late night party), take a break when you want and nap at 3pm if you feel like. No questions would be asked. No formal clothing to be worn; imagine working in a t-shirt and shorts. So this could mean goodbye business suits and ties, shirts and skirts. Also, you don't have to bother about being presentable. Do you need any more reasons in the convenience department? And when working is convenient, a happy and a contented space is created.

Cost Effectiveness – Working from home will give you complete relief. No more you would be fretting over the rising in the cost of fuel? You don't have to drive to work anymore. And even if you are pursuing freelance writing as your secondary vocation, you can write anywhere and everywhere. You can shape up your article while sitting in a coffee shop; or may be proofread and mail your ready assignment to your client right from your office cubicle! And those who would choose to be a full time freelance writer, they no more would need to pay the baby sitter. Why would you need a baby sitter, now that mommy or daddy is at home!! Imagine how much money you can save by working from home.

Flexi Hours! Flexi Work!– How many times were you asked to work late, just when you decide to go for a dinner date with your partner? There are times you promise your kids you will take them for soccer practice but that's the day your boss needs you to reach work early. Guess what, when you work from home, you don't have to think of all this. Attractive income can be earned and then take a vacation for a week, no questions asked. You don't have to be apologetic if you want to take a day or a week off. Just make sure all your pending assignments are complete and take up the next lot of work when you think you can start writing again, and you are set to go.

Adding to Knowledge Base- Another great thing about being a freelance writer is it helps you increase your knowledge base tremendously. There will be requests/jobs to write about topics and subjects that you weren't aware of but then suddenly you will find yourself researching about it and in the process, learning and understanding about them. It can be asserted that you will be a knowledgeable person when you take up freelance writing as a career option for yourself.

If you possess the required skills to become a freelance writer, you are better off becoming one rather than being stuck in the rut of being answerable to someone else on a scheduled program. Well, these were some of the pros of working from home. But then again, if we say there are no cons and portray a rosy picture; we would be lying. As every yin has a yan, there are a few consequences of working from home.

Here Are Some Of The Common Ones:

Unpredictable Income – Unlike a full-time job, there is no guarantee of a fixed paycheck when you are self-employed. But then that doesn't mean it will always be low than what you make in your job. Many a times, you will earn much more. However, the income could not be consistent, especially during initial tenure of freelance writing. One cannot, and must not, assume to be earning a handsome money right from the day one. That is the risk you will have to take when you jump from a secured job to becoming self-employed.

Complacency – You tend to get complacent when you work for yourself. You tend to take yourself for granted, especially when you are not answerable to anyone else. This can be lethal for your business. You need to show the same determination and responsibility that you had when you were working with an organization. If not, you will not achieve your goal and also lose a few clients due to your careless attitude.

Overworking– This can happen if you are determined to make it big as soon as possible. If you take your job too seriously and don't give life a chance, you will be overworked by the end of the day. This may lead to mood swings and also impact the work life balance. When you work for a regular company, you have fixed hours of operation, which leaves you with ample time for family life and a personal life. Don't let work take over completely. Strike the right balance and give a chance to life as well.

These are some of the cons of working from home. But of course you are smart enough to make a decision whether the pros work in your favor, or the cons can make a difference to your schedule and work life balance.

Chapter 2: Qualities Needed To Be A Successful Freelance Writer

There are several specific qualities and skill-sets that are mandatory for taking up freelance writing. One thing you should remember, freelance writing is more a skill based job than a will based job. If the fundamental skill is missing and there is absence of will to learn the skill, then chances are you will not exactly make a full-fledged career out of it.

Apart from the basic requirement of strong linguistic skills; perfect grammar and punctuation, you need to have mastery on the following qualities and skills:

Flawless Communication – You need to be an excellent communicator to become a decent writer. After all, writing is nothing but communicating through your words. There are different types of writers; some prefer direct and to the point writing, some others prefer a conversational tone; while there are some others who prefer a formal tone. You need to be able to communicate and cater to every type of audiences and clients to become a successful writer.

Playing with Words - You need to have a way with words that are fairly simple, but that offer a character to your writing. Use words that strike a chord and impart a unique personality to them. The reader should be able to connect to your writing. You also need to be a story teller who can capture the attention of the reader.

Fertile Imagination - Your writing will be as good as your imagination but then of course your research would matters too. To be able to communicate with the reader and spin your words, you need the right imagination that will help your words sound more convincing. Allow your imagination to run wild when you start writing and let it take over. Your ideas need the wings of words to become worthwhile publishing content.

Creative Courage– You need to have the courage to put your thoughts on paper and be prepared for rejection. Very few freelance writers start off with f.ying colors. Initial rejection is a part and parcel of being in the freelancing world. Do not get upset on being turned down Get up and start writing once again. If things don't work in your favor, brace yourself and try again. Your aim should be to try till you finally succeed.

Discipline - You need to be controlled and disciplined about your work because it becomes easy to get carried off when you work for yourself. It is important not to get distracted and stay focused on work. A lot of freelancers get complacent knowing that they are their boss and are not answerable to anyone for their work;

they tend to take it easy. But remember, it will be bad for your business because, at the end of the day, you are still working for clients who expect you to follow deadlines.

Apart from the above listed points, you need to keep a vigilant and a wide eye for these as well –

- Zero spelling mistakes
- Meticulous Research
- Proofreading of the document before submission
- Crisp editing for any errors
- Maintaining lofty quality standard
- Adhering to client's guidelines
- Providing value for money

⁇

Chapter 3: Etching a Career Out of Freelance Writing

Freelance writing can be made a lucrative career provided you have the skill and the will to perform. Take a deep thought what your idea of a Career is. For most people, a career means:

- A job that gives them satisfaction
- A job that helps them earn money
- A job that helps in growing and maturing as a person

- A job that gives you a feel good factor about what you do and how much you derive out of it.

If your definition of a career matches with these examples above, then freelance writing is a worthwhile career option for anyone who can write and communicate effectively. Here is how you can make a suitable career out of freelance writing.

Job Contentment – You will not take up a writing job unless you have an aspiration to become a writer. You won't give up on your regular job for a freelance writing job unless writing lures and tempts you. Writing will be impossible unless you have the right kind of creative juices churning inside you.

Money making– If you establish yourself (which is not very difficult for those having writing talent in them) into freelance writing, there is no limit to what you can earn. You will be able to earn money if you find the right clients and are dedicated to earning a specific amount on a daily or weekly basis. If you set yourself a target and work towards achieving it, there is no holding back from making a good earning out of freelance writing.

Creative Growth – As we mentioned earlier, you can learn a lot in life by becoming a freelance writer because you will constantly be researching on various topics. Your knowledge (though theoretical) about different topics will grow on a daily basis and chances are you will learn or increase your understanding about a new topic on a daily basis. This will help you grow and diversify as a person. You would be able to hold up an intelligent conversation and create good content.

These reasons will give you encouragement and confidence for your career choice. It will also help you earn the money you deserve. You will always be looked upon as a smart and an intelligent individual by family and peers (coming from personal experience).

Earning Big Bucks

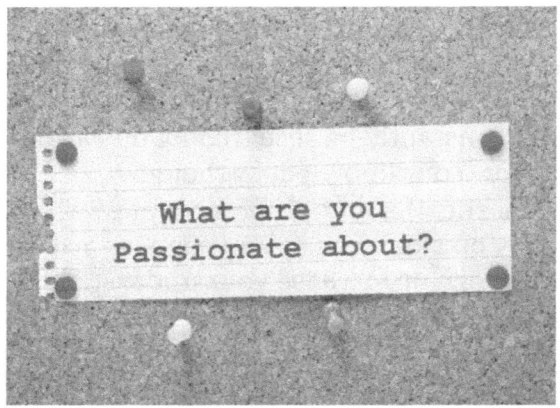

Again, let us be the ones to break it to you, yes absolutely!! Plenty of money can be earned as long as you establish yourself as a good writer. To start with, you can always sign up with freelance content writing websites. Initially, there will be a lot of competition that you will have to face. But then what is life without some competition!! Initial make a mark and then there won't be any dearth of work.

Hunting for Big Clients and Quality Work Of course, if you have to move to the big league and start earning at least $25 to $40 per hour, you will have to make certain sacrifices. Of course, you will have to prove yourself with the quality of your work to get bigger and better paying clients. Once done, don't settle for any less than your value. If you maintain the good quality of work, clients will not think twice before paying you for quality work. Everyone understands that high-quality work = high payout, so never compromise on quality if you want to get a higher payout.

Never take up Low Paying Jobs

Most of the freelance writers commit this mistake. When there is not enough work, try not to work for cheaper rates, unless of course you need the money desperately. If you take up a low-paying job as a writer, chances are you will get stuck in the rut of these low paying clients all your life and not be able to make any substantial income. On the other hand, it will ensure that you get constant jobs and will get you a paycheck every week. A decision is to be made whether you want a steady paycheck, or you want to work with people who will pay you more as per your caliber.

Broaden your Horizons as a Writer

The beauty here is you will earn as a freelance writer. If you work as per either option, you will still end up making money. The question here is how long you have to work to earn a decent income because if you target high paying clients, you will have to work for a limited time. But if you work for the smaller fish in the sea, you will have to slog for nearly double the time to earn half as much as you normally would.

Chapter 4: The Beauty and Perks of Freelance Writing

When you make any career change, it is advisable to tread carefully. Though you should take certain risks in life, but it is always preferred to be safer than sorry. So if you are thinking about making a switch from your full-time job to become a freelance writer, it is best to test the waters first. You have to be open about the fact that not everyone has the skill to become a writer. Sometimes the reality is different than what you think it is.

Self-Assessment

You may consider yourself to a writer material but maybe you need to hone your skills. This is not for discouraging you from taking the big step; we are just preparing you to face the competition with preparedness. Get a reality check done and find out whether it is a sensible decision to make a career out of writing or you are imagining an impossible feat. Initially, start as a part-time freelance writer. You can test your caliber as a writer as well as have an alternate source

27

of income for yourself. If the boat sails smooth, you have explored newer career options for you. But if you don't do well or if you don't enjoy the experience, you always have the cushion to fall back on. You can go back full time to your job or search an alternate career option for yourself.

Be Practical and Realistic

You need to consider the fact that writing cannot be a career choice for everyone. Just because someone else you know clicked doesn't mean you will too. In the same manner, just because you don't know any personal success stories about successful writers doesn't mean there aren't any. Assess your capabilities if you are cut out to become a writer. Don't go on what you feel or think. Try yourself out and determine your strengths and weakness.

The good thing about the world of freelance jobs is there is no shortage of work. Apply for those tasks you think you can do justice to. Even if you are not a rage in beginning, don't give up. Keep on striving harder and take an apt decision.

You may be successful, or you may not, but don't get deterred by one bad experience and also don't get carried away by one good experience. Take it one day at a time and go slow. Persistence is the major key and with time you will get the hang of the freelancing world. After gaining sufficient experience, you will surely start making some money for yourself.

Making a Graceful Transition

The high paying jobs out there don't come so easy. You need to establish yourself as a skilled and a dependable writer to make a mark for yourself. Once done you will start raking in the cash, but till then keep working diligently to get there.

Freelance writing is not a ticket to earning fast and easy cash. You need to work hard and relentlessly. Build a portfolio, gain some experience, build a client base, improvise on your skills and eventually you will get there. When you feel you have achieved it, then it will be a good time to take the plunge, and make writing a full-time career for yourself. And believe us; once you reach that stage, there is no looking back for you. You will meet many lucrative opportunities and establish your career.

Chapter 5: Meet Success As A Freelance Writer

To become a freelance writer, you don't just need basic writing skills. You need to learn and master the tricks of the trade as well. The freelance writing industry is an extremely competitive and highly dynamic. For you to make a place for yourself in that space, you need to lean and understand the main attributes of being a successful freelance writer. These are the qualities that differentiate a good freelance writer from an average.

Commitment & Perseverance – As a freelance writer, you need to have an absolute commitment towards quality; and perseverance to sustain it. You need to ensure that the work you submit is of the highest quality. Ensure that there is no compromise on the language and the grammar. You may be perfect with your writing skills, but there may be typo errors and need to proofread. Ensure that you check for such uncalled errors before it is submitted to the client.

Timeliness – There are millions of good freelance writers out there. All writers have the skill to write and the will to perform and shine. What differentiates a good writer from a perfect writer is the one who is extremely punctual on submitting his assignments. Your self-employed status should respect the client's deadlines. If you are not professionally punctual, chances are that the client would pull back his business from you and look for another writer who can deliver assignments on time.

Research & Development– When you are assigned a specific topic don't write to just complete the project. Write to add value to the subject. The reader should not need any more information once they read your content. Your research on the topic should be meticulous and should sound as if coming from a subject matter expert. Make sure that the figures, facts and the quotations you use are accurate, and you pay attention to detail.

Professionalism – Be professional with the clients you work and treat them with importance because that is where your work assignment and paycheck will come from. Don't take anyone for granted in terms of quality, deadline, and the content. Remember, a satisfied customer will always come back for more business. That is exactly what you need for a flourishing career in freelance writing.

SEO – You may not understand the importance of search engine optimization (SEO) initially, but when you decide to become a freelance writer, remember SEO is the Mantra to live by. You should understand the importance of SEO, keywords, back linking, keyword density, etc. to work as a freelance writer.

If you understand the importance of these attributes and focus your work on them, there will be plenty of good work around.

Remember persistence is extremely important in the freelancing world. Give your absolute best, and eventually success will be yours.

Chapter 6: Some Freelance Writing Sites

Yes, it is true that there is ample work out there for a freelance writer. There are millions of clients who need content for their business on an everyday basis. But where do you find these clients? Often, the writers and the clients don't know how and where to get in touch with each other. One of the ideal ways is to assign work through freelance writing websites that gives access to work as well as has a workforce under same portal. Here are few of the best websites available for freelance writers where they can meet some real clients and make some real money.

Elance.com – This is one of the best websites to find requests for writing assignments from around the world. This is also a perfect forum to reach the best writers from around the world. As a writer, you have access to infinite working opportunities, but you will have to compete it out with other freelancers from across the world. You will have to submit a bid along with a proposal. You should be able to cite why you are the best candidate for the job. The client will review your profile and decide which bidder is the best suited for the job and will award the project accordingly. In terms of payment too, Elance is one of the best and the safest site. As soon as your project is completed, you will get paid for the same. Client will also give a feedback and a score. Your scoring will help you bag newer projects from newer clients.

Iwriter.com – Brad Callen's website Iwriter.com is again a perfect platform for new freelancers to earn a quick buck. This site has unique working much differently than the other freelance working websites. There isn't any kind of competition to bid for the job. Once you register, you can start working within a minute. You choose a project, start working, complete it within the allotted time and wait for the client to approve or reject it based on the quality of your work. There are several clients who assign work on a daily basis, and there are unlimited work opportunities for a writer. The pay scale also increases as your expertise increases.

Freelancer.com – Freelancer.com is another site that is similar to Elance in its way of working. As a writer, you will have to bid for projects, and if the client accepts your bid, you will have to submit the project within the allotted time. The rest of the dynamics of this site is similar to Elance and is a good way to earn money as a writer.

Some of the other sites like www.odesk.com, www.vwriter.com, www.guru.com, and www.writingbids.com, etc. also feature writing related jobs. Until you form a strong client base, it is best to rely on these sites for jobs as it will ensure you get a steady stream of work and income too.

Most of the time, you meet long term clients on these forums. Once a client is satisfied with the quality of work you provide, they too would want to continue professional association with you. Hence, we stress on the fact that the quality of work is extremely important. If people are happy with your work, only then will they continue to work with you. So if you want a client to repeat his order, give him the level of expertise and quality he is seeking.

Beware Of:
The mad world of Freelancing can become a little out of control because you might step out to get some work for yourself. But stay aware, you might end up becoming a scapegoat. There are many predators on the prowl for novices who will do just about anything to bag a project. You need to keep away from these scammers or else instead of making an earning, you might lose your time, money and effort.

Here Are A Few Things You Need To Remember While Searching A Job -

- Never sign up with a website that requests you to pay a fee upfront before assigning a job
- Never agree to work for free for someone who promises you work later. Your work and charity are two different things. You are here

to earn and not for helping others to earn from your skills

- Work with sites that can provide payment protection or else you are on your own.
- Genuine writing websites do not charge a joining fee; they always share a percentage of your earning AFTER you start earning.
- It is important for you to keep these things in mind before you start hunting for a freelance writing assignment for yourself.

Chapter 7: Bagging High Paying Project Without Bidding

Yes, we just told you that most of the freelance writing websites ask for bidding for the projects listed on them. And this bid-fight could be someone established and experience, thus minimizing the chances of zeroing of your bid. Of course, the competition is enormous, and you might feel frustrated in the beginning. We can positively say that most new freelancers don't land a project in the first week of bidding unless they drastically slash their rates and agree to write for peanuts. You don't want to do that because that would get you nowhere...perpetually nowhere. Wouldn't it be great if work just came by without you having to fight for it? Well, of course, yes, and tell you what, it is possible too. But for that you need to be an established writer with whom clients have worked in the past and are satisfied with the quality of the work. They should have some reason to come back to you with more projects. But is that enough? How long will an old client be able to keep paying the bills? There have to be newer sources and clients who need to hire you for your work.

So in this section, we will discuss how a freelance writer can bag writing assignments without having to bid on content mill sites. Yes, there are quite a few ways you can achieve that. But then you have to understand that you might not be able to generate revenue while you are trying. But consider this lull as a silence before the storm because when this works out in your favor, you will NEVER have to worry about getting other work again.

Here are some smart tips on bagging new clients without going through cut throat competition on bidding sites and content mills.

Start Blogging – You need to have some online presence where you can showcase your work and portfolio. The client needs something to purview before they come to you with work. The best way is to blog regularly, but you can even create a website or publish your content to spread the word about your work. Keep the blogging professionally compliant so that it provides value and information to the reader. Showcase your best work on the blog because if you need someone to hire you for your work, they should like what they see.

Define Your Forte – Make a rule to keep away from the herd mentality and create a niche for yourself. You need to ensure that the client understands what kind of writing services you excel at. You can be good at sales copies, landing pages, blog posts, EBooks, newsletter writing, online content, SEO, etc. The client should not have to assume or guess where your strength lies. Give value to the details.

Highlight whatever you feel you excel at. You should be able to furnish samples to the client if they particularly want to review your past work.

Crisp Content – Showcase how different you are from other freelance writers by educating and motivating the client to hire your services. It is important to do case studies and offer value to the reader so that they understand how assigning their business to you will add value to their business. They need to understand that you have the required expertise for them to trust their business with you.

Contact Me Section – On your blog or website, there has to be a special 'Contact Me' segment so that prospective clients, who are influenced by your work, can contact you. Be subtle and avoid being brash in pushing for your services. The idea is not to sell, but to convince them to hire you. If you can achieve that, it will help you command a better price and be on the right end of the bargain.
Promotion – Social Media, newsletters, forums, backlinks, etc. are a good way to get people talking about your work. Don't waste your time waiting for clients to

walk in without any marketing effort. In today's world, you are as successful as you want to be seen as, so market yourself accordingly.

These are some of the suggested ways to get you noticed. And once you do get noticed, a consistent work track will strengthen your portfolio. If a client likes what you have put forth, the work will come to you on its own. Keep the mantra of Quality and rest will fall into place.

Chapter 8: Desperation Strictly Not Allowed

The first rule of being a new freelancer – to sustain coolly and patiently through dry period when there might be less or no jobs or assignments. Of course, this isn't, for those who have established themselves well and have a steady source of assignments. While striving to find writing assignments, you will face times when there is no work. Like the saying goes 'An idle mind is a devil's workshop' you will start doing things out of desperation. The trick here is to avoid getting too desperate and simply focus on bagging quality assignments.

Desperation may lead you towards -

- Working for peanuts
- Losing focus
- Coming across as a needy person, who is in no position to bargain
- Evasive mindset leading to lean self confidence

All these aspects can drive away a potentially high payer. Never come across as desperate and needy. Your portrayal of having no work assignments would solidify their notion about your lack of talent. This should be avoided at all costs. When you face a shortage of work, you need to pull your act together and start working towards overcoming the desperate attitude and come across as your usual confident self. Believe in your caliber and stop panicking. Everyone has a rough patch; this is yours. Your mettle as a person will shine through if you can come out of this situation and make a fresh start.

Get out of the rut and change the situation

Aggressive Marketing– Don't get complacent and lose hope. You need to market your skills more aggressively now. It is important you trust your abilities before somebody else who has to put his money on you. Since you have free time on hand, use it wisely and start promoting your skills and work. Take this chance to ensure that the potential client sees you as an asset and not as a liability for his business. Remember, when you have a steady work flow again, you might not be able to market yourself the same way. So make the best possible use of time in hand.

Maintain Positive Attitude– It may sound like a cliché but a rough patch is just that, a rough patch. It will pass ultimately. Don't let a dull moment get to you. Maintain a positive attitude and approach other work prospects with the same attitude. In all likelihood, don't leave a bad impression on your client. Be in control of the situation and make the best of the opportunity you get, because that's your first chance to get out of the 'no work' rut.

Never Give up Writing – One of the common reactions of freelance writers during the lean work patch is that they tend to develop negative thoughts in their minds and contemplate the idea of giving up the writing. This is in fact one of the gravest mistake they make. Instead, make a wiser and an optimal use of your time. This is the time when you can update some good posts on your blog and attract some more clients to your profile. Maybe these blogs won't pay you now but they will strengthen your portfolio. You have free time on your hand, use it wisely. Giving up writing will wash down all your efforts made so far and would bring you back to where you started from.

Connect – Connecting with other writers is an important aspect of a freelance career. Since the freelancer himself of herself has to create its client base, professional connection becomes must. Keep in touch with other writers and be cordial enough to get references through them. Move in compliant circle so that the right kinds of people interact with you and you get noticed by strategic clients. Connecting this way may not fetch you instant results but it will surely build up a platform for you for benefits in the longer run.

Chapter 9: Right Mood and Mind to Create Good Content

Writing is not like driving a car or operating a machine. You cannot start the ignition or switch on to start writing. Mind should be fresh and correct frame to write. You need the right focus to start writing. As a writer, you will always be in situations when you will not be able to think or come up with ideas. During such times take control of the situation and create the right kind of mood to weave magic into words.

Following Are The Tips To Condition Your Mind And Create The Content That Sells -

Keeping Faith & Confidence in Yourself
– Just because you get stuck when writing something doesn't mean you are not a good writer. Do not forget that you are a good writer to get the work assignment in the first place. Every writer faces writer's blockade once or a while. Get the understanding that it isn't the end of the world and stop moving around with an apologetic state of mind. As a start you can start reading one of your best works, something that you are immensely proud and satisfied of. If you could write that, it means you are capable of writing just about anything under the sun. Have faith in your abilities and stay upbeat.

Write What You Are Best At - If you don't feel like writing on the topic that is assigned to you, write something you would enjoy writing. Whatever your mind thinks of, keep writing. This way you will relax mentally and get back in the writing mode. If that doesn't work too, take a break. Watch the television, read a book or just cook, or whatever that you think can help you feel relaxed. Once you feel fresh enough, start writing again and create the magic.

Settle a Deadline – Most writers work very well on deadlines. Maybe you are one of them, so get started and set you against time. The time-bound principle may help in making your mind work in a better way so try that. Maybe the results of the same can be much better than writing in a relaxed environment.

Shift your Work Place– If nothing else works, just move away from where you usually work and try a different place. A change in setting will help to calm your nerves and relax your mind. You can try sitting in the living room, on the dining table, in the backyard or just about any place that will get your creative juices flowing. A change in usually setting does the trick when everything else fails.

Do not work ad-hoc – Here ad-hoc refers to working in smaller spurts and not with complete focus. One of the common drawback of working as a freelancer is that we tend to do many things at the same time. For example, a work-from-home mom would prefer writing an article while she is cooking some dish. It is very much likely that she would set her laptop at the kitchen table and would have half of her mind over the dish that is cooking over the stove. This way, she would not be able to focus completely over the writing. Hence ad-hoc writing should be avoided. Rather, set a segregated time for writing when household chores or other activities will not bother you.

Remember this, when you take up a job you are responsible for completing it. Once in a while it is OK to not complete it but don't make that a habit. For having a steady stream of clients, punctuality would play an important part in retaining them. Of course quality is the bottom line but no one likes to work with a person who has a careless attitude. Own up to your work assignment and complete the same in a responsible manner.

Chapter 10: Networking: Way To Surge Ahead

Marketing yourself is extremely important because only you and your skills are responsible to get you more work. A major part of marketing is networking with like-minded people who are in the same business as you are. Effective communication is one important skill you should possess as a freelancer. You need to connect with relevant people and network for the right ideas. But before that, have a clear understanding of networking.

Understanding The Importance Of Networking

Networking may sound like a big thing but, in a nutshell, it is nothing but building relationships with relevant people. Network with people who can be potential clients, vendors, or someone who can publicize your work. Networking can be pretty tedious if not handled the right way. One thing about networking is that it will seldom yield instant results. The wait can stretch to months or even a couple of years to see some profitable results. It may sound frustrating, but the fact is networking is one of the best strategies for freelancers. However, you have nothing to lose while you are networking. All that you have to do is invest your time interest and effort. Once you would be visible and acknowledged in the right circle, you would enjoy meeting and connecting with like-minded people.

Types of Networking

Networking can either be face to face or over the web. For face to face networking, you will have to connect with peers, organizations, attend conventions or meet up with like-minded people who have the same interests as you. In terms of online networking - LinkedIn, Facebook, Twitter etc are some of the most globally used platforms. Nothing is definite for which type of networking will work. It can differ, so it is best to indulge in both kinds so you can reap the benefits of both worlds.

Networking Strategies

There are various types of networking strategies that you can use, so that you can market yourself and your skills appropriately. Some of the most common networking strategies are -

Build and maintain a networking contact list – This will work where you can build a prospective customer base. Stay in touch with potential clients whom you have met and discussed work in this line of business. A contact list will help you stay on top of things. Do not force your presence on others. Rather, keep yourself genuinely interested in your circle.

Right Tools for Face to Face Networking – When you meet people in organization or forums, you need to create an impressive mark on meeting them. It is also important that they have means to get in touch with you at a later time. Do not fail to hand out your business card, a copy of your portfolio or brochures that describe the services you offer. Don't forget that networking has to be always continued with a follow up.

Exude Confidence – Making a first impression is extremely important, especially during face to face interaction. Dress formally and remain crisp in your interaction with your clients. Don't be over confident about your skills, stay positive, often smile and give attention to detail. You should come across as a professional whom the client can rely on.

Be a careful listener – When the client speaks, don't listen to merely reply or answer. Listen to understand what he has to say and what he needs from you. A good listener is always appreciated. Ask questions or clear doubts whenever you feel like, but keep them at the end of the conversation and avoid interrupting people when they are talking. Being a careful listener will teach many implied things that can only be understood with deep and inherent thinking.

Give an impressive presentation whenever possible – To portray your expertise and authority in your field, it is best to volunteer for a presentation. Ensure that the clients are interested to hear you out; don't force your ideas on them. Do your homework and avoid fluttering in front of the client. However, for this you must be prepared. Try not to come up with impromptu presentation as their will be chances of goofing up.

Connect Online – It is important to grow your network, so connect with people via online forums like LinkedIn and Facebook. Online presence has its own charm and benefits. Connect online with other freelance writers and clients. But keep a periphery of your interaction and avoid getting personal with prospective clients. Online connectivity will also keep you updated over what latest is happening and how to get upgraded.

Pay attention to the other person's needs – If a person connects with you, he or she will also have an agenda to market or network themselves. They will have similar needs like yours, so don't make it all about you. Let the other person speak as well. Exchange ideas and thoughts, you will only enhance your knowledge from that.

Be Consistent and Regular – If you use social media to connect, don't be around for a day and go missing for a couple. You need to be constantly active and in-touch to become a successful networker. It may just take about 20 minutes of your time per day, but use it wisely. An inactive profile may not be good for your business.

If you manage all these aspects of networking, you will build a strong and an effective network, consequently leading to growth of your writing business.

Chapter 11: Secrets of Becoming a Successful Freelance Writer

Every business has certain principles that it flourishes on. In the same manner, Freelance writing as well as other professions have a set of principles that are extremely eminent for its growth. Here are some important principles to achieve success as a freelance writer.

Don't Compromise on Price – After all we work for the money. You have a skill; you command a certain price for the service you provide. Do not take a pay cut, especially if you are sure of your quality of writing. Don't bottleneck yourself by limiting your preferences. Don't compromise on the price, especially on content mills or to win a bid. You are likely to get stuck in a rut of low paying jobs, once trapped.

Customer is King – Treat your client the way he wants to be treated. Give him quality service to earn a conviction. Remember, a happy customer will come back to you. Make sure you provide him with everything he needs and you will never see any dearth of work. Once a rapport will get established further work will become easier for you. Rather he will also refer your services to others.

Get a Head Start on the Assignment – Never become too complacent about your work. A lot of people wait for the end moment or the near-deadline to begin work. This is bad for your business. The moment a project is assigned to you, get working on it. A prompt head start of the project will take you to a comfortable finish. This would also give you sufficient time to complete project and revise it thoroughly.

Understand what the client wants –
Though you are the expert in the matter, the client is putting his money on you. His input matters a lot in executing the project. Ask the right questions and talk about the client's content needs. Clear all your doubts and understand what his ideas and requirements are. Do not overlook clients' instructions and never to try to supersede clients' version. You may be right in your own terms but follow what client wants. You can definitely present your suggestions but final say should abide to what client wants.

Focus on Long Term – A client may start with a small project, which may not seem financially lucrative but the same client can be a potential long term client if you offer him good quality content. It is now a well-known modern adage and indeed the bottom line of the writing world. If you are getting paid to write, make sure you deliver the absolute best content. If you focus on getting clients for a longer run, there will never be a dearth of work and you won't have to bid on projects and compete for paltry sums with other writers.

Networking is crucial – We have already established that networking is extremely important for a freelance writer. Build a strong network with prospective clients, vendors and people who might need your services. Nothing works better for your business as a satisfied client and word of mouth publicity. Networking will also prevent your stagnation as a writer. You would know newer people and newer avenues would be available to you.

Effective Time Management – Always take enough work to keep you busy but avoid taking more than you can bite. Don't commit to different clients about completing their projects on priority if you cannot do it. Never sublet your work because that will break the clients' trust. Rather try and ask for an extension and get the quality work done. This will ensure the quality remains high and also maintain an open channel of communication and trust with the client.

Treat your Business as a Real Job – Don't be careless about your work just because you are your boss. Display commitment and responsibility to shine amidst your competitors. Remember that your business needs the same attention or more, than you showed when you were employed for someone else. It is your name that is at stake here after all. Maintain daily discipline lest your assignments would pile up enormously.

These are some important principles that will give your freelance writing career the right kind of push to grow. Following these principles will give you confidence and establish your faith in your skills. All these would come back to you in the form of more and better business. Eventually, you would meet success after success.

Chapter 12: Avoid These Mistakes

As a freelance writer, you will make a lot of mistakes when you start your journey. However, if you begin your journey by learning the mistakes that most other writers make, you can avoid repeating them. Learning from others mistakes is the biggest learning. Below listed are some of the common mistakes made by new freelance writers that must be avoided them at all costs.

Charging Less than Your Worth – Yes we know we have covered this, but it is important you understand and realize your worth. If someone is paying you for your service, it means you are an expert, and you know better. That also means that you need to be paid as an expert and not a paltry sum that you can do without. Understand your worth and make sure you are paid accordingly. The point is to maintain your standard right from the inception of your freelance writing career.

Not Maintaining a Work-Life Balance – Most freelance writers assume that they can work when they want and relax whenever they want to. But the fact is, once you commit yourself to a project, it is important to complete it first within the deadline set. Don't get too complacent, it can be extremely bad for your business. Punctuality is extremely important if you want to be successful as a freelance writer; else regular clients will dodge you.

Getting Carried Away with Work – There may be many freelance writers who think nothing more than their business and only keep working. They lose their work-life balance and feel mentally lethargic. This leads to shoddy or poor quality work. Depression may also seep in, if they are unable to find enough work to keep them busy. It is extremely important to set specific working hours each day and stick to the schedule. Anything more or less once in a while is OK, but if you make a habit out of it, your work will suffer in the longer run.

Dreading Failure – It is alright to fail; no one is perfect. Strive hard for coming out of the failure. If you fail once, it doesn't mean you are no good. Rather, need to do better than before. Failure to better your efforts, might fail you again. So accept the fact that failure can always be overcome by efforts. Moreover, being a freelancer will always keep things in your hand. In case any assignment fails and gets rejected, you can always learn from your mistakes and move on with a wiser approach.

Fabricating Sub-Standard Content – Don't be one of those writers who are too conscious about word count and not the quality of the content that they create. Fabricating fluffy and phony content is an absolute no-no, unless of course if you are writing a fictional tale or a novel. People will subscribe to your writing when it helps them learn and understand. You need to bring forth the facts that should be highlighted. Do not fabricate a story just to sound good. That is called being a scammer!! You are paid to research and write, and you should do exactly that. When you do that, you also add a lot of value to your intelligence.

Procrastinating– Do not delay in starting to write soon after you bag the project. Unnecessary procrastinating can cost you plum projects. This may also lead to fear and mistakes. Keep ample time in your hand and don't be afraid to experiment with research and writing styles, as long as you are determined to improve further.

Checklist

On a concluding note, ensure that you have followed the fundamentals of freelance writing. Here are some dos and the don'ts, to be followed before you embark on your journey as a freelance writer. If you follow these basic rules, you will find the success that you are seeking to become a high profiled freelance writer.

Here is a checklist of aspects you should remember all times to become a successful freelance writer:

- Quality – Quality – Quality
- Content is King
- Be Punctual
- Don't get too complacent, be responsible for your business
- Focus on the client's needs when writing a copy
- Don't underestimate your talent
- Charge as per your value, don't lower your price and dignity
- Remember you are the Subject Matter Expert
- It is alright to falter once in a while
- Learn from your mistakes

If you ensure compliance to these basic aspects, you will not falter from achieving your goal of being an accomplished and a successful freelance writer.
⁇

CONCLUSION

As discussed in this eBook, freelance writing is a very rewarding career option for those who have the basic writing skills along with the will to learn and evolve. But before you take a leap of faith, it is best to have a backup plan and then go full-fledged in the field.

In this eBook, we have covered almost every relevant angle and aspect that you can experience as a freelance writer. Knowing these will give you an upper hand so you can avoid making some of the common mistakes that most freelance writers make. Not just that, you will also learn the tricks of the trade from those who have found success being a freelance writer.

Before you take the plunge, set a goal for yourself. What do you seek in this profession? Are you in for the money? Are you in for the creative satisfaction? Are you in because you don't want to sit idle at home? Are you in because you want to do something significant in life? Whatever your reason is to turn to this profession, make sure you work towards achieving it because being a freelance writer can help you become and achieve all of these things.

This is your chance to prove yourself, to believe in the skill that you possess and also earn at the same time. Many around the world are making millions as freelance writers. Take a step and join the bandwidth to make a mark in this industry. It is now your time to create content that can be read, understood and appreciated globally. And because you have read this far, it could mean that you always wanted to learn and be one of them.

One thing is assured, if you put your skills to work and your mind to writing, there is nothing that can come between you and success. Without much ado, it is time now to take the first step towards realizing your dream of becoming a freelance writer.

Happy Writing!

www.ingramcontent.com/pod-product-compliance
Lightning Source LLC
Chambersburg PA
CBHW070932180526
45168CB00003B/1044